Ray Palmer

Hymns of my Holy Hours

and other pieces

Ray Palmer

Hymns of my Holy Hours
and other pieces

ISBN/EAN: 9783337286668

Printed in Europe, USA, Canada, Australia, Japan

Cover: Foto ©Lupo / pixelio.de

More available books at **www.hansebooks.com**

HYMNS

OF MY

HOLY HOURS,

AND OTHER PIECES.

BY

RAY PALMER.

NEW YORK:

ANSON D. F. RANDOLPH,

No. 770 BROADWAY.

1868.

EDWARD O. JENKINS, PRINTER,
20 NORTH WILLIAM STREET, NEW YORK.

To My Sister,

MRS. ANGELINA PALMER GRINNELL,

THE PLAYMATE OF MY CHILDHOOD, AND THE DISINTERESTED AND CONSTANT FRIEND OF MY RIPER YEARS, THESE PAGES

ARE INSCRIBED,

AS A SLIGHT EXPRESSION OF THE PROFOUND AFFECTION AND GRATITUDE OF HER BROTHER,

RAY PALMER.

PREFACE.

———◆———

THE writer has had such evidence, from many sources, that a small volume of hymns, published by him some time since, has proved a grateful offering to fellow disciples, not only in his own communion and his own country, but also in other branches of the Church of Christ and in other lands, that he has been encouraged to make this small additional contribution to the hymnology of his time.

Only a part of the following hymns are suitable to be sung. The remainder are designed to give expression in hymnic form, to the deeper emotions of the devout soul in its various moods, experiences and disciplines. How necessary it is that hymns intended to be used in worship, should be simple and unadorned, should so preserve unity of thought and feeling as to seem artless, and to be easily apprehended, it is evident from current criticism is even now but partly understood. Hymns intended chiefly for reading, however, allow a far greater variety of thought and measure, and may take a much wider range. If the following lyrics express truly the healthful emotions of one Christian heart, they will be certain, it is believed, to awaken response in others. Should they assist the faith and love of any in finding fit utterance before God, the highest wish of the author will have been fulfilled.

The writer feels obliged to add, that if the compilers of Manuals for Public Worship shall desire to introduce any of these hymns into their Collections, he cheerfully consents, provided always that the hymns be taken exactly as they are. He repeats, even with greater emphasis than in the preface to the former volume, his protest against the alteration, or abridgment, of the hymns of a living author, to adapt them to the uses or the taste of others, without his consent. He cannot but regard it as a breach, not of courtesy alone, but of Christian morality as well.

R. P.

CONTENTS.

ADDITIONAL PIECES.

PRAISE TO CHRIST.

King of Kings and Lord of Lords.—Rev. xix. 16.

O CHRIST, the Lord of Heaven, to Thee,
  Clothed with all majesty divine,
Eternal power and glory be,
  Eternal praise of right is thine!

Reign, Prince of Life, that once thy brow
  Didst yield to wear the wounding thorn ;
Reign, throned beside the Father now,
  Adored the Son of God first-born !

From angel hosts that round Thee stand,
  With forms more pure than spotless snow,
From the bright, burning seraph band,
  Let praise in loftiest numbers flow !

(9)

To Thee, the Lamb, our mortal songs,
　　Born of deep, fervent love shall rise ;
All honor to thy name belongs,
　　Our lips would sound it to the skies.

Jesus !—all earth shall speak the word ;
　　Jesus !—all heaven resound it still ;
Immanuel, Savior, Conqueror, Lord,
　　Thy praise the Universe shall fill.

THE SOUL'S CRY.

I cry unto Thee daily.—Psalm lxxxvi. 3.

OH, ever from the deeps
    Within my soul, oft as I muse alone,
Comes forth a voice that pleads in tender tone ;
    As when one long unblest
    Sighs ever after rest ;
Or as the wind perpetual murmuring keeps.

    I hear it when the day .
Fades o'er the hills, or 'cross the shimmering sea ;
In the soft twilight, it is wont to be,
    Without my wish or will,
    While all is hushed and still,
Like a sad plaintive cry heard far away.

    Not even the noisy crowd,
That like some mighty torrent rushing down
Sweeps clamoring on, this cry of want can drown :

But ever in my heart
Afresh the echoes start ;
I hear them still amidst the tumult loud.

Each waking morn anew
The sense of many a need returns again ;
I feel myself a child, helpless as when
I watched my mother's eye,
As the slow hours went by,
And from her glance my being took its hue.

I cannot shape my way
Where nameless perils ever may betide,
O'er slippery steeps whereon my feet may slide ;
Some mighty hand I crave
To hold and help and save,
And guide me ever when my steps would stray.

There is but One, I know,
That all my hourly, endless wants can meet ;
Can shield from harm, recall my wandering feet ;
My God, thy hand can feed,
And day by day can lead
Where the sweet streams of peace and safety flow.

THE LOVE THAT STOOPETH.

What is man, that Thou art mindful of him ?—PSALM VIII. 4.

MY God, though far above my thought
    The wonders of thy being rise ;
Though earth itself appears but naught,
    And all the orbs in yonder skies
Seem trifles while I think of Thee,
Yet Thou dost deign to visit me !

Lord, what is man ?   Ah, not to him
    Is due thy coming down to dwell ;
Thou whose high praise the seraphim
    Touch their entrancing lyres to tell ;
Thou comest for no worth of mine,
'Tis all of grace and love divine !

And I may speak, as speaks a child
    That gazes on a father's face
Suffused with love, serenely mild,

And fair with tenderness and grace ;
May lift my eyes without a fear,
And know that, speaking, Thou wilt hear.

Thou wouldst not that my needy soul,
　For what might ease its inward pain,
From clime to clime, from pole to pole,
　O'er the wide world should seek in vain ;
Should burn with deep, intense desires,
As one consumed with hidden fires.

Thou bidst me come my thirst to slake
　At the full fountains of thy love ;
And Thou my soul dost fill and make
　Content and glad like those above ;
For with thy gifts enriched and blest,
My search is o'er, and found my rest.

MIDNIGHT WORSHIP.

At midnight I will rise to give thanks unto Thee.—Psalm cxix. 62.

"O UNSLEEPING! ever keeping
   Faithful watch about my bed,
O'er me bending, and defending
   From all ill my weary head ;
Now each restless thought composing,
And in peace these eyelids closing,
   Father, keep my soul," I said.

Thou didst hear me, Thou art near me,
   Waking at this midnight hour ;
Changing never, loving ever,
   Thou art my defence, my tower ;
Thoughts of Thee dispel all sadness,
Thoughts of Thee give strength and gladness,
   And I rest upon thy power.

Purely glowing, stars are throwing
　　Glad rays through the solemn night,
Ever gleaming, as if beaming,
　　With thy glory on my sight;
By their order and their beauty,
Thou dost teach me love and duty,
　　Bid me shine with virtue's light.

Praises bringing, upward springing,
　　Mounts my quickened soul to Thee;
Hope fulfilling, passion stilling,
　　Thou dost come, my God, to me!
And in holy, sweet communing,
All my noblest powers attuning,
　　Thou dost teach me thine to be.

Nightly waking, from me shaking,
　　Slumbers soft, I will arise;
Bowing lowly, O Most Holy,
　　I will lift to Thee mine eyes;
So shall speed my warm devotion,
Winged by tender, pure emotion,
　　Upward through the midnight skies.

Ever living, ever giving
   Life and joy to all thine own ;
Interceding, as once bleeding,
   Priest and Lamb before the throne ;
Thou my prayer presentest ever,
Thou my praise refusest never,
   Christ, I trust in Thee alone !

So while praying, calmly saying
   " Father, bless me from above !"
So believing and receiving
   Gifts of grace and smiles of love,
I again mine eyelids closing,
And till dawn in peace reposing,
   All thy faithfulness shall prove.

2

MORNING WORSHIP.

My voice shalt Thou hear in the morning, O Lord.—PSALM v. 3.

FATHER, while the shades of night
  Fly before the crimson dawn,
Heavenward speeds my soul her flight,
  Gladdened by the day new born.

Nature, fresh enrobed and fair,
  Greets me with her kindly smile,
And I breathe the fragrant air,
  Drinking in thy love the while.

All thy works are full of Thee!
  Glows my heart with living praise ;
Lowly bends the reverent knee,
  Upward waiting eyes I raise.

While from garden, field and grove,
  Morning carols wake around,
Swift my thoughts ascend and rove
  Where eternal songs resound.

With the wide creation's choir,
　My rapt soul would chant her hymn,
Kindling with the holy fire,
　Of the burning seraphim.

Light of men, when forth shall break
　Thy full splendor, dimmed so long,
Earth one hymn of praise shall wake,
　Ages the glad strain prolong.

Son of God, Redeemer, Lord,
　All thy goodness none can tell;
When thy gifts I would recall,
　High as heaven the numbers swell.

Through all labors of this day,
　Let thy hand sustain me still;
Through all perils guard my way,
　Make me strong to do thy will.

Let my day dawn calm and bright,
　Where no eye forever weeps;
Where forever comes no night,
　Where eternal sunshine sleeps.

EVENING WORSHIP.

At evening-time it shall be light.—ZECH. XIV. 7.

COME, Jesus, with the coming night,
　　Refresh and cheer my weary heart;
At evening-time it shall be light,
　　If Thou art near, though day depart.

Welcome this shade that brings release
　　From hurrying labor's noise and strife;
That calls from restless thought to cease,
　　And calms the throbbing pulse of life.

From tedious toil, from anxious care,
　　Dear Lord, I turn again to Thee;
Thy presence and thy smile to share,
　　Makes every burden light to me.

With Thee, of all sad thoughts beguiled,
  Peace nestles in my tranquil breast ;
And like a pleased and happy child,
  In thy kind arms I sink to rest.

Till night's dark watches all are gone,
  O faithful Shepherd, guard my sleep,
And when yon mountains greet the dawn,
  Give strength my heavenward way to keep.

THE HOUR OF JOY.

Thou hast put gladness in my heart.—PSALM IV. 7.

ALL things to mine eyes are bright ;
Throbs my heart with deep delight ;
Birds pour forth delicious notes,
Fragrance on the still air floats,
Earth and heaven seem full of gladness,
And my soul forgets all sadness,
Glows and quivers with the thrill
Of the joy that doth it fill.

Swift-winged thought exults to range,
Fancy, as with magic change,
Makes e'en ugliness look fair,
Finds fresh beauty everywhere ;
Life itself is one pure pleasure,
Tasted without mete or measure ;
Of whate'er could make her blest,
My glad soul seems now possest.

Upward, upward, strong and free,
Borne on wings I seem to be ;

Unconfined by earthly bars,
Soars my spirit to the stars ;
E'en beyond the starry regions,
Filled with orbs in countless legions,
Mounts she with untiring wings,
Mounts and evermore she sings.

Whence this ecstasy divine ?
Why so rapt this soul of mine ?
O my God, with warm desire
Thou didst set my heart on fire ;
Then thy love and goodness showing,
And thy light around me throwing,
Thou didst give Thyself to me,
Thou hast made me glad in Thee.

Thou art of all joy the crown ;
Thou with joy canst sorrow drown ;
Let me drink forevermore
At the well-spring running o'er ;
In thy smile is sadness never,
In thy smile is gladness ever,
To thy child, O Father, give
Ever in thy love to live !

DE PROFUNDIS.

Out of the depths have I cried unto Thee, O Lord !—PSALM cxxx.

IN the dark days of grief,
    When the dull hours drag wearily
      and slow,
When from the brimming eyes hot tears do flow,
  Where, where to find relief,
    Shall the bruised spirit go !

I see the world rush on ;
Each, passion-stirred, intent to reach his end ;
All, nerved for life's high prizes to contend,
    Glide by me and are gone ;
    No healing can they lend.

Voices of mirth I hear ;
But these chase not the gloom thick brooding o'er,
Nor calm the billows that about me roar ;
    They jar upon mine ear,
    And wound me but the more.

I look on Nature's face,
'The groves, and summer fields, and lawns and
   streams,
All beautiful as visions seen in dreams ;
   But Nature's smile and grace
   To mock my anguish seems.

The silent woods I tread,
Where aisles invite with oak and beech o'erhung,
And sweet wild notes by many a bird are sung ;
   The still cool paths I thread,
   But yet my heart is wrung.

To friendship's breast I fly ;
Of its deep tenderness I own the power,
More gently throbs my brow for one short hour,
   But ere my tears are dry,
   Falls a returning shower.

O Jesus, Thou hast wept ;
When faithful hearts mourned o'er a brother
   dead ;

For mortal griefs thine own pure tears were
    shed ;
        And ever Thou hast kept
        Kind watch o'er hearts that bled.

Since Thou art Love Divine,
And deep compassions in thy bosom glow,
This heart whose anguish Thou alone canst know,
        Would all to Thee resign,
        And trust Thee though laid low.

My spirit Thou canst heal ;
Canst give me patience while I wait for light,
Bid cheerful day smile on my starless night,
        And peace canst make me feel,
        While yet tears dim my sight.

On Thee, O let me lean ;
As if on thine own bosom let me weep,
Till restless sorrow there is lulled to sleep—
        Sleep gentle and serene
        If Thou my slumber keep.

To joy then shall I wake,
And. taught new trust, with constant, loving
    heart,
To Thee shall cling, nor bear again to part,
    Till heaven's bright dawn shall break
    And bring me where Thou art.

THE CROWN.

There is laid up for me a crown.—2 TIM. IV. 8.

THE crowns of earth are jewelled dust,
    Or weights, the wearer's brow to press ;
But Thou, O Christ, dost give the just
    A nobler crown of righteousness.

That crown, of thine own love the seal,
    On thine a gift of love bestowed,
Diviner splendors shall reveal
    Than e'er on princely head hath glowed.

Ten thousand faithful souls and true
    Now wear the crown, that wore thy shame ;
That many a wasting anguish knew,
    And as through fires to glory came.

We yet must wage the long drawn strife,
    And oft with prayers our groans ascend ;

We battle for immortal life,
  Give strength and courage to the end.

Then be it ours to hear Thee say,
  When we shall lay our armor down—
"The faith ye kept! Ye won the day!
  Come, take and wear the matchless crown!"

BURDENS.

Cast thy burden upon the Lord.—PSALM LV. 22.

EVER as I onward go
   Through the mazy round of life,
  Days and years with struggles rife,
Wearily I tread and slow ;
Oft my spirit falters, faints,
Oft breathes out her sad complaints.

Guilt's huge burden weighs me down,
   Pressing heavily and sore ;
   Till thy face, dear Lord, no more
Glows with smiles ; Thou seem'st to frown,
Though I long thy grace to prove,
Though I know that Thou art Love !

Oft thou chafest, haggard Care !
   Wearing, wasting, day by day,
   Thou each rising joy dost slay

That my soul would upward bear ;
Thou dost clog my heavenward flight,
Spoil my spirit of her might.

Leaden Grief, thou pressest hard,
    When have sped the shafts of fate,
    When my heart bleeds, desolate,
And by many an arrow scarred ;
When on sorrow's sea long tost,
All the lights of hope are lost.

Dark thou broodest o'er my soul,
    Gloomy Doubt, when hidden lie,
    Locked in awful mystery,
God's deep counsels, and the scroll
Sleeps unopened till the time
When goes forth his word sublime.

Thou, O spectre-loving Fear,
    All too oft hast o'er me flung,
    Terrors that like rocks have hung,
Sinking every thought of cheer ;
Till a ship I seemed to be,
Foundering in the far-off sea.

Yet I hear a Father's voice :
    " I, Jehovah, am thy strength ;
    All thy burdens bring, at length,
Cast on me—then go, rejoice !
Make thy days with songs resound,
Rest in holy peace profound !"

Yes, my God ; away—away
    Haunting unbelief and gloom !
    Vanish, and for joy give room,
Joy of faith, while now I pray ;
Henceforth sweetly on thy breast
Love Eternal, will I rest !

A PRESENT GOD.

In thy presence is fulness of joy; at thy right hand there are
pleasures for evermore.—PSALM XVI. 11.

SMILE, O my God, on me ;
  Thy presence let me feel ;
My soul thy glory longs to see,
  Thyself in me reveal.

I would not wait for Heaven ;
  Heaven may begin below ;
To every new-born soul 'tis given
  A present God to know.

The vision of thy face
  Fresh life and joy inspires ;
While o'er my spirit flows the grace
  That kindles all her fires.

Though on my saddened heart,
  The gloom of night should lie,
3

Faith shall not fail nor hope depart,
   If I but feel Thee nigh.

When earth's fleet years are past,
   And I no more shall roam,
Give me, my God, to find at last
   With Thee my changeless home.

Then shall my blessed soul,
   At fountains gushing o'er,
While circling ages ceaseless roll,
   Drink pleasures evermore.

THE VISION OF CHRIST.

Then face to face.—1 CORINTHIANS XIII. 12.

O CHRIST, I long to know Thee
  As Thou art known above ;
Long, face to face, to show Thee,
  In faultless praise, my love ;
But Thou thyself now hidest
  Beyond my feeble sense,
Though all my steps Thou guidest,
  Thine arm my sure defense.

O'erpowering is the splendor
  About the unveiled throne ;
Where bright archangels render
  A service all their own ;
That glory sight confounding,
  Those wonders rich and rare,
The anthems high resounding,
  This mortal could not bear.

Yet Lord, to see Thee, pining,
    In thought I oft ascend,
And where thy hosts are shining,
    I, too, before Thee bend ;
As one in rapture dreaming,
    Celestial bliss I feel,
And in that moment's seeming,
    Glow with a seraph's zeal.

When from this dream awaking,
    A weary pilgrim still,
Sloth from my spirit shaking,
    With fixed, unfaltering will,
My soul in courage stronger,
    Holds on her toilsome way,
Content to watch yet longer,
    Till dawns the wished-for day.

THE COMFORTER.

I will send Him unto you.—JOHN XVI. 7.

O HOLY Comforter,
  I hear
Thy blessed name with throbbing heart,
Pressed oft with sorrow, sin, and fear,
And pierced with many a venomed dart;
  Come, Messenger divine,
  Come, cheer this heart of mine!

O Holy Comforter,
  I know
Thou art not to dull sense revealed,
Thou com'st unseen as the sweet flow
Of the soft wind that woos the field;
  Breathe, Messenger divine,
  Breathe on this soul of mine

O Holy Comforter,
Thy light
Is light eternal and serene ;
Shine Thou, and on my ravished sight
Visions shall break of things unseen :
Come Messenger divine,
Make these bright glimpses mine !

O Holy Comforter,
Thy love
O'erfloweth as the flooding sea ;
Give me its tenderness to prove,
Then shall my heart o'erflow to Thee ;
Come, Messenger divine,
Fill Thou this breast of mine !

O Holy Comforter,
Thy grace
Is life and health and hope and power ;
By this I can each cross embrace,
Can triumph in the darkest hour ;
Come, Messenger divine,
The strength of grace be mine !

O Holy Comforter,
Thy peace,
The peace of God, impart and keep
Unruffled till life's tumults cease,
And all its angry tempests sleep ;
Come, Messenger divine,
Thy perfect peace be mine !

THE PLACE OF PRAYER.

Enter into thy closet.—MATTHEW VI. 6.

O EVER sacred spot,
   Where clamor cometh not,
Where earth may be forgot,
And peaceful stillness undisturbed may reign;
   I joy that I may know
   Such holy calm below,
   Nor feel life's restless flow,
When thy sweet solitude well pleased I gain.

   While lowly here I kneel,
   My God, thy love reveal,
   And give thy child to feel
A Father's blessing falling on his head;
   I see thy smile benign,
   I hear Thee call me Thine,
   For Thee I all resign,
And evermore would by thy will be led.

Hither, O Christ, I flee,
That I by faith may see
Thy face unveiled to me,
And all the secrets of my heart may tell ;
May lean upon thy breast,
Lull all my fears to rest,
And,—joy of joys the best,—
Hear thy loved voice known to my soul so well.

Tell Thou my longing heart,
Dear Lord, that mine Thou art ;
Then all afresh shall start
The tears of grateful tenderness and love ;
Give me that precious stone
That bears a name unknown,
The pledge that Thou wilt own
And make me to behold thy face above.

Oft as I enter here,
Great Comforter, be near
My wrestling soul to cheer,
Let thy best gifts and graces all be mine :

In Thine own perfect light,
O give me visions bright
Of things beyond my sight ;
Fill my whole being with the life divine !

AT THE CROSS.

I am crucified with Christ.—GAL. II. 20.

O JESUS, sweet the tears I shed,
    While at thy cross I kneel,
Gaze on thy wounded, fainting head,
    And all thy sorrows feel.

My heart dissolves to see Thee bleed,
    This heart so hard before ;
I hear Thee for the guilty plead,
    And grief o'erflows the more.

'Twas for the sinful thou didst die,
    And I a sinner stand ;
What love speaks from thy dying eye,
    And from each pierced hand !

I know this cleansing blood of thine,
    Was shed, dear Lord, for me ;

For me, for all—O grace divine!—
  Who look by faith on Thee.

O Christ of God! O spotless Lamb!
  By love my soul is drawn ;
Henceforth forever thine I am,
  Here life and peace are born.

In patient hope the cross I'll bear,
  Thine arm shall be my stay ;
And Thou, enthroned, my soul shalt spare,
  On thy great judgment-day.

THE VOICE OF CHRIST.

Peace—be still.—MARK IV. 39.

AMID the darkness, when the storm,
   Swept fierce and wild o'er Galilee,
Was seen of old, dear Lord, thy form,
   All calmly walking on the sea ;
And raging elements were still,
Obedient to thy sovereign will.

So on life's restless, heaving wave,
   When night and storm my sky o'ercast,
Oft hast Thou come to cheer and save,
   Hast changed my fear to joy at last ;
Thy voice hath bid the tumult cease,
And soothed my throbbing heart to peace.

But ah ! too soon my fears return,
   And dark mistrust disturbs anew ;

What smothered fires within yet burn!
  My days of peace, alas, how few!
These heart-throes—shall they ne'er be past?
These strifes—shall they forever last?

I heed not danger, toil, nor pain,
  Care not how hard the storm may beat,
If in my heart thy peace may reign,
  And faith and patience keep their seat;
If strength divine may nerve my soul,
And love my every thought control.

O may that voice that quelled the sea,
  And laid the surging waves to rest,
Speak in my spirit, set me free
  From passions that disturb my breast;
Jesus, I yield me to thy will,
And wait to hear thy "Peace, be still!"

SUBMISSION.

Thy will be done.—MATTHEW XXVI. 42.

THY holy will, my God, be mine ;
  I yield my all to Thee ;
No more shall thought or wish repine
  Whate'er my lot shall be.

Thy wisdom is a mighty deep,
  Beyond my thought thy grace,
My soul shall lay her fears asleep,
  Secure in thine embrace.

When clouds and darkness rule the hour,
  Thy bow on high I see ;
And e'en the rending tempest's power,
  Shall work but good for me.

At every step mine eyes shall turn
  To watch thy guiding hand ;

My dearest wish shall be to learn
   And do thy pure command.

On Thee I rest my trusting soul
   Thou wilt not let me fall ;
Though surging billows o'er me roll,
   I shall be safe through all.

Grant me, my God, at last to hear,
   Well pleased, the call to die,
And 'mid the shades, with vision clear,
   To see my Saviour nigh.

Then when thy glory breaks on me,
   All radiant as the sun ;
Be this the joy of heaven—to see
   Thy will forever done!

ALONE WITH CHRIST.

I will come to you.—John xiv. 18.

ALONE with Thee! Alone with Thee!
O Friend divine!
Thou Friend of friends to me most dear,
Though all unseen I feel Thee near,
And with the love that knows no fear,
I call Thee mine.

Alone with Thee! Alone with Thee!
Now through my breast
There steals a breath like breath of balm,
That healing brings and holy calm,
That soothes like chanted song, or psalm,
And makes me blest.

Alone with Thee! Alone with Thee!
Thy grace more sweet
Than music in the twilight still,
Than airs that groves of spices fill,
4

More fresh than dews on Hermon's hill,
My soul doth greet.

Alone with Thee! Alone with Thee!
In thy pure light
The splendid pomps and shews of time,
The tempting steeps that pride would climb,
The peaks where glory rests sublime,
Pale on my sight.

Alone with Thee! Alone with Thee!
My softened heart
Floats on the flood of love divine,
Feels all its wishes drowned in Thine,
Content that every good is mine
Thou canst impart.

Alone with Thee! Alone with Thee!
I want no more
To make my earthly bliss complete,
Than oft my Lord unseen to meet;
For sight I wait till tread my feet
Yon glistering shore.

Alone with Thee!   Alone with Thee!
    There not alone,
But with all saints, the mighty throng,
My soul unfettered, pure and strong,
Her high communings shall prolong,
    Before thy throne.

THE CONSENTING HEART.

Come unto me.—MATH. XI. 28.

YES, kind Saviour, grieving
    O'er the sad past,
All my vain hopes leaving,
    Come I at last;
        Thine—thine I am,
        O bleeding Lamb;
To thy heart receiving,
    Hold Thou me fast.

On thy word relying,
    Safe let me rest,
All my tears now drying
    On thy dear breast;
        Dawns the sweet day,
        Bright o'er my way,
Foes and fears all flying,
    Here I am blest.

All my footsteps heeding,
  Shield me from ill,
In green pastures feeding,
  By waters still ;
    Always with Thee,
    Lord, let me be ;
Thou all kindly leading,
  Thine be my will.

When—life's last day ending,—
  Dark death is nigh,
Jesus, o'er me bending,
  Note my last sigh ;
    In that dread hour,
    Strong in thy power,
On swift wing ascending,
  Home let me fly !

THE VICTORY OF FAITH.

Thanks be unto God that giveth us the victory through our Lord
Jesus Christ.—1 CORINTHIANS XVI. 57.

WHY should these eyes be tearful
    For years too swiftly fled ?
And why these feet be fearful
    The onward path to tread ?
Why should a chill come o'er me
    At thoughts of death as near ?
Or when I see before me
    The silent gates appear ?

Behold my Savior dying !
    I hear his parting breath ;
Entombed I see him lying,
    A captive held of death ;
Yet peacefully he sleepeth,
    No foe disturbs him now,
And love divine still keepeth
    Its impress on his brow.

But lo ! the seal is broken !
   Rolled back the mighty stone ;
In vain was set the token
   That friend and foe should own ;
The weeping Mary bending,
   Sees not her Savior there ;
But sons of light attending,
   A joyful message bear.

The Lord is risen !—He liveth
   The first-born from the dead ;
To Him the Father giveth
   To be creation's head ;
O'er all forever reigning,
   Of death He holds the keys,
And hell—his might constraining—
   Obeys his high decrees.

Flies now the gloom that shaded
   The vale of death to me ;
The terrors that invaded
   Are lost, O Christ, in Thee !

The grave, no more appalling,
   Invites me to repose ;
Asleep in Jesus falling,
   To rise as Jesus rose.

Oh, when to life awaking,
   The night forever gone,
My soul, this dust forsaking,
   Puts incorruption on ;
Lord, in thy lustre shining,
   In thine own beauty drest,
My sun no more declining,
   Thy service be my rest !

NOCTURN.*

Enter into thy closet, and shut thy door.—MATTHEW VI. 6.

I SIT in my silent chamber,
    And my spirit mounts in thought;
Dear hour of divine communion,
    That oft a deep joy hath wrought!
And lo! as in holy vision,
    The heavens unfold above,
And there fall bright beams of glory,
    There is breathed the breath of love.

I see, through the amber portal,
    The angels of God descend;
'God's Host'—they are swift of pinion,
    And ever his saints attend;

* I have thought it best to insert this piece here, because it is hymnic in its spirit and is in keeping with what has gone before. It is however rather a night meditation than a hymn.

I hear the celestial chorus,
　　Harps touched with divinest skill,
Tones sweeter than breathing zephyrs,
　　That on my hushed soul distil.

The praise of the Holiest hymning,
　　The skies with the song resound ;
The stars seem to join their voices,
　　As they float in the dark profound ;
And the loving Father of spirits,
　　Though ruling all worlds the while,
To the 'Sons of God' doth hearken,
　　And sheddeth on them his smile !

Ay, Lord, thou bendest yet lower ;
　　The voices of earth dost hear ;
Dost catch each sigh of contrition,
　　Dost note each glistening tear ;
My praise is to thee as incense,
　　For prayer thou returnest grace ;
Not now may these eyes behold thee,
　　But I feel thy blest embrace.

Why—why should I envy seraphs,
  That they stand so near the throne,
If here thou dost deign to meet me,
  If here dost thyself make known ?
If now in these evening shadows,
  This stillness of dying day,
My soul may drink of thy fulness
  Till won from her griefs away ?

My God, thy secret is with me,
  A secret I ne'er can tell ;
'Tis life, 'tis peace, 'tis a rapture,
  When with me thou com'st to dwell ;
While the twilight shades grow deeper,
  As spreadeth her wings the night,
On me there falleth thy splendor,
  And all is serenely bright.

My finite and feeble spirit
  With thine the Infinite blends,
Till with Heaven's own bliss o'erflowing,
  Her weary, vain quest she ends ;

As if on thy bosom lying,
  She findeth her wished-for rest,
By Eternal Arms enfolded :
  Have ye more than this, ye blest?

Ah yes, ye spirits immortal,
  Ye are not to sense confined ;
No law in your faultless being,
  When ye long to soar, doth bind ;
And I too, at length ascending,
  From sense forever set free,
Shall God-ward cleave the bright azure,
  As glad and as pure as ye !

My feet shall tread the fair city
  Adorned as a beautiful bride ;
Shall come to the living fountains,
  And walk by the crystal tide ;
To the loved again united,
  Once lost amidst tears and pain,
I shall know the full affection
  For which I have yearned in vain.

I shall then, with undimmed vision,
　See what had been hid before ;
From wonder onward to wonder,
　Forever mount up and adore ;
If on earth thy works have charmed me,
　What raptures shall fill me there,
When I gaze on spotless beauty,
　Than all I had dreamed more fair !

Oh, then on the throne whose brightness
　Outshineth yon blazing sun,
The Head of the whole creation,
　I shall see the Crucified One !
Where night spreads no more her shadow,
　I, amidst the ineffable glow,
Shall live on his smile forever,
　And ALL THAT HE IS SHALL KNOW !

Additional Pieces.

THE SEA-SIDE.

I SIT beside thee, murmuring sea,
   And watch thy ever changeful motion;
Note where soft clouds float over thee,
   And where commingle sky and ocean;
White sails are scattered here and there,
   Of swift ships o'er thy bosom gliding,
That in the hazy, shimmering air,
   Move dream-like on the wave dividing.

I mark where on yon pebbly shore,
   Along the crescent bay far-sweeping,
White waves are breaking evermore,
   E'en when the winds are calmly sleeping;

I gaze when storms are on the deep,
　　Like unchained demons wildly roaming,
When billows huge their tumult keep,
　　In frantic fury madly foaming.

Thy deep and still abysses, where
　　Dwell life and beauty all-abounding,
Where pearls are born and mosses rare,
　　And sea-flowers bloom, the rock surrounding;
The countless mysteries concealed,
　　Down where thy lowest vales lie hidden,
Seem oft as if to sight revealed,
　　While thought treads paths to sight forbidden.

Yet, mighty sea! 'tis not the glow
　　Of thy broad face when calm and smiling;
'Tis not thy wrath when heavenward go
　　Thy surges into mountains piling;
'Tis not the secrets of thy breast,
　　Thy countless marvels all unspoken,
That make me with thee ever blest,
　　Held long as by a spell unbroken!

'Tis that thou stirrest in my soul
　　Thoughts all too deep and vast for telling ;
Thoughts free as thine own waves that roll
　　On and yet on with ceaseless swelling ;
'Tis that emotions, memories, loves,
　　And buried joys, thou dost awaken ;
Flown hopes dost call, like nestling doves,
　　Back to the heart too soon forsaken.

'Tis that far o'er thy wide expanse
　　I know that sunny lands are lying,
And at thy side, full oft, perchance,
　　To those fair climes my thought is flying ;
I scent the orange groves afar,
　　I see the tufted palm-tree spreading,
I rove where orient gardens are,
　　In endless bloom their perfumes shedding.

'Tis that in years far, far away,
　　When youthful pulses high were beating,
I joyed by thee at eve to stray,
　　True hearts in high communion meeting :

5

And now thou givest back once more
   The faces whose bright smiles have perished .
I see them, greet them, as of yore,
   Though lost, in faithful memory cherished.

'Tis that when on thy strand I feel
   A reverent tenderness come o'er me ;
Am moved by thy gray rocks to kneel,
   With all thy grandeur spread before me,
And breathe my worship in His ear
   Who in his greatness thought out-reaching,
Is ever to the lowly near,
   The glory of his goodness teaching.

'Tis that by thee I feel the love
   That, like thy floods, no measure knowing,
From the eternal fount above
   To mortal man is ever flowing ;
And hear His footsteps who of old
   Sublimely trod the troubled billow,
Who with a word the storm controlled,
   Rising majestic from his pillow.

'Tis that, at sight of thee, inspired
   With conscious power, my soul ascending,
Shoots high her flight with wing untired,
   Her heavenward yearning impulse lending,
Till fairer visions greet her sight
   Than charm where tropic suns are gleaming :
Realms bathed in uncreated light
   From God's high throne forever streaming.

Long as my mortal years shall roll,
   Grand Sea ! thy sights and sounds shall cheer
       me,
Bring calm sweet musings to my soul,
   And God and kindred spirits near me ;
Then, when these eyes behold no more
   Thy noble face, its charm still keeping,
O let thy long loved solemn roar
   Be as a requiem o'er me sleeping !

BURIAL HILL.*

ON Plymouth's Burial Hill we trod,
    And high each heart was beating ;
It seemed indeed " the field of God,"
    Each stone his praise repeating.

'Twas not mid chill December's blast
    O'er sea and land wild sweeping ;
June's longest day—too soon 'twas past—
    Its carnival was keeping.

Soft skies were o'er us as we stood,
    With summer zephyrs breathing ;
We saw God's smile on field and wood,
    And flowers the earth enwreathing.

---

* The most interesting moment in the session of the late National
Council of the Congregational Churches was that when, standing on
Burial Hill at Plymouth over the graves of the Pilgrim Fathers, its
members solemnly reaffirmed, with prayer and singing, their fidelity
to the system of Christian Faith from which those noble men drew
their highest inspiration.

Beneath our feet the Pilgrims slept.
  The brave, the true, all lowly,
Their humble graves by angels kept ;
  The ground to us was holy.

Ah ! then all tenderly we thought,
  We thought with pride and wonder,
How—Freedom's price divinely taught—
  They stood unflinching yonder :

Though wintry chillness reigned around,
  And wintry winds were howling,
Though only savage man was found.
  And savage beasts were prowling.

Anew we felt their hopes and fears,
  When want and sickness wasted ;
As through the lingering, weary years,
  Of sorrow's cup they tasted.

Grand souls ! that with heroic will
  The waves of trouble breasted ;
Not e'en did woman falter, till
  Beneath that turf they rested !

For God, for truth, for man, they bore
  Loss, exile, grief, and danger,
As Christ, the Lord they loved, of yore
  Accepted earth's low manger.

And there above their sacred dust
  Whose names shall never perish,
We vowed THEIR FAITH, a holy trust
  For all mankind, to cherish.

O God, who heard'st our prayer and song
  'Neath heaven's high dome ascending,
Bid us in thine own might be strong,
  For that pure Faith contending.

From regions wide where Plenty fills
  Her lap to overflowing ;
From rugged realms where rocks and hills
  With gold and gems are glowing ;

From northern lakes that cool and bright
  Their sparkling waves are spreading,
To where fresh orange groves delight,
  Perpetual fragrance shedding ;

From all the wide, wide land, the cry
  For God's good Word is speeding :
And Freedom lifts her hands on high,
  No more enchained and bleeding !

O wake, ye sons of Pilgrim sires !
  Go, live in power and beauty
The life sublime their Faith inspires ;
  Its watchword—GOD AND DUTY !

MOUNT WASHINGTON.

HERE let me gaze in silence. Awed, en-
　　tranced,
And stilled as if to worship reverently;
Moved to all thoughts most noble, pure, and
　　calm,
To the strange heart-thrills which the vast
　　awakes,
I seem o'ermastered by a mighty spell:
Exalted, yet subdued, my heart I yield,
In this rude solitude, to eye and ear.
Beauty and grandeur and a sense of God,
Commingled all, enchant my willing soul,
Stir it to longings vague and infinite,
Fill its profoundest depths and hold it charmed,
In tranquil wonder and sublime delight.

Ye massive domes, ye towering cliffs and crags,
Ye purple summits that lift up your brows

Bathed in pure azure, or enwreathed with clouds,
Far, far ye rise above our mortal paths—
Paths resonant with groans and wet with
    tears ;
And, in soft sunshine glowing, now ye smile,
As if exulting in a living joy ;
As if in ever-peaceful, grand repose,
Ye feel not the rude shocks that shake the world,
Heedless though battles rage and kingdoms fall.
Yet know I well that ye not ever thus
Serenely stand ; that oft around your heads
Fierce tempests rave and cleaving lightnings
    gleam,
And thunders peal that from each rifted gorge
To gloomy skies are echoed awful back.
Changeless ye seem, as if in giant might,
Defying elements and hoary time,
'Twere yours the flow of ages to abide,
While man and his proud works are turned to
    dust.
And yet I mark that ye bear countless scars ;
That down your rugged steeps torrents have
    swept

Gashing your sides, and avalanches plunged,
Baring your rocky breasts to sun and storm.
Exult not proudly o'er frail, mortal man,
That naught for him endures ; ye too at last,
By earth's fixed, unrelenting law, shall waste.
Yet shall your term be long.   Man oft shall mourn
His perished hopes and joys ; shall weep full oft
His heart's best treasures ravished all too soon ;
Shall see his laurels fade, his honors die,
His empires pass, his palaces decay,
His canvas mould, his marbles crumble down,
His noblest words of eloquence and song
Lost in forgetfulness, and known no more ;
While yet unchanged your majesty remains.
Oh ! ye are worthy, venerable forms,
That on the long-gone centuries have looked,
And wait to look on ages yet to come,
Of the deep reverence that my spirit feels.
Helpful ye are to lift my heart to Him
Whose hand of old your strong foundations laid,
And piled, with power almighty, your huge towers.

Therefore I love to climb your rocky steeps,
To note each outline, drink the spirit in
That breathes through all your glens and forests
     wild ;
To feel the influence of your changeful moods,
And gain from each some joy or impulse new.
I love, as now, to watch with you alone,
When morning greets you early with her smile :
When evening bids you late a kind good-night !
When ye are holding converse with the stars,
At midnight clustering thick around your heads,
Like jewels in some august monarch's crown.
I love among the pines, far down your slopes,
When winds breathe softly in the cool, still eve,
To linger for the latest notes of birds—
Notes sweetly tender as befits the hour ;
While rills and distant waterfalls respond,
And with their chimes the diapason fill.
Ah ! then I seem with God, and almost hear
Voices Celestial speaking words of love.
And lingering still, well pleased, I dare to dream
That the soft cadences that swell and die
In your thick shades, are harmonies divine

Wafted to earth from holy choirs of heaven ;
Or greetings kind of saintly souls from whom
Long since I parted at the gate of death ;
Who, loving and well loved, were wont to speak
Words that were ever music to my ears.

Long it were joy to stay.   But now again,
To duty's call attentive, I return,
As if from holy ground, to meet the shock
Of life's rude jars, and wrestle with its ills.
But from your base, O mountains ! I shall go
Stronger, with loftier purposes inspired,
With fresher thoughts and calmer life within,
And firmer rest in God.   His changeless pledge
Of love, and love's best gifts to faithful souls,
Shall stand when even ye, crumbled by time,
And lost by slow decay, shall be no more,
And earth itself hath vanished as a dream.

MISANTHROPY.

O WORLD, to some so bright and fair,
Thy charms I cannot see ;
Thy joys—thy purest, choicest—are
But hollow joys to me.

When all around look blythe and gay,
And every heart is glad,
I turn in weariness away,
In spirit sore and sad.

Not e'en the fireside's kindly cheer
Can smooth my knitted brow ;
In that which once I prized so dear
I find no pleasure now.

Farewell, ye pomps of life ! farewell
Ye pageants all untrue !
Scenes 'mid which others joy to dwell
I bid ye glad adieu !

Where nature blooms in beauty pure
   My footsteps now I bend,
There, unmolested and secure,
   A life of peace to spend.

Be mine the hermit's lonely cot,
   Round which the wild flowers wave,
And there, unheeded and forgot,
   Be mine his lonely grave.

RESPONSE.

AND think'st thou, fool, when thou hast fled
   The busy haunts of men,
That thou shalt find thy passions dead,
   To waken not again ?

Think'st thou thy soul's deep craving, felt
   Without thy wish or will,
When thou hast by thy pallet knelt,
   Shall evermore be still ?

The warm affections in thy breast,
  That keenly thirst for love,
Think'st thou that these can lie at rest,
  Content no more to rove?

The conscious power for noble deeds,
  That wakens high desire,
Think'st thou, when thou hast told thy beads,
  'Twill stir no inward fire?

The sense of duty that commands
  To do with all the might,
When thou shalt fold thy idle hands,
  Will this forswear the right?

The thought of deeds of love that thou
  Shouldst every day have done,
Will it not haunt when thou shalt bow,
  As nightly sets the sun?

The world's great agonising cry,
  From suffering millions wrung,
Will that for thee in silence die
  When thou hast vespers sung?

The dread of reckoning strict and stern
   For unused gifts and powers,
Will that not in thy bosom burn,
   Through all thy lonely hours ?

Ah, fling thy fatal dream aside,
   Stand forth in manhood true ;
Where life's great battle rages wide
   Be strong to dare and do !

In virtue's conflict stern and high,
   Thy soul shall grow divine ;
In triumphs, joy shall light thine eye,
   And holy peace be thine.

With splendor then shall close the day
   That ends thy mortal strife ;
Men by thy grave shall pause and say—
   " He lived a noble life ! "

THE CHORUS OF ALL SAINTS.

[Suggested while hearing Haydn's Imperial Mass.]

THE choral song of a mighty throng
   Comes sounding down the ages ;
'Tis a pealing anthem borne along,
   Like the roar of the sea that rages :
Like the shout of winds when the storm awakes,
   Or the echoing distant thunder,
Sublime on the listening ear it breaks,
   And enchains the soul in wonder.

And in that song as it onward rolls,
   There are countless voices blended :
Voices of myriads of holy souls
   Since Abel from earth ascended ;
Of patriarchs old in the world's dim morn,
   Of seers from the centuries hoary,
Of angels who chimed when the Lord was born—
   " To God in the highest, glory !"

6

Of the wise that, led by the mystic star,
  Found the babe in Bethlehem's manger,
And gifts, from the Orient lands afar,
  Bestowed on the new-born stranger ;
Of Mary, the blessed of God Most High ;
  Of the Marys that watch were keeping
At the Cross where He hung for the world to die,
  And stood by the sepulchre weeping.

The voices of holy Apostles rise,
  The symphony grandly swelling,
And land to land with the strain replies,
  As they go of Messiah telling ;
And with them the martyr host conspire,—
  A host as the stars for number,—
They sing from the rack and from out the fire,
  From the dust in which they slumber.

From the saints obscure, that in every age
  Have fought the good fight unheeded,
Whose names ne'er graced the historic page,
  Who thought not of fame, nor needed,

Come tones that tell of a tender love,
　Of a spirit calm and holy ;
Oh, sweet to the ear of the Lord above
　Is the praise of the meek and lowly !

He hath heard, well pleased, when the psalm
　　　awoke
Dark caves and the dismal prison ;
When the stillness of lonely glens it broke,
　Or on damp night-winds has risen ;
When up from the cot of the poor it came,
　Or from meanest cabins stealing,
'Twas an offering dearer than altar's flame,
　The love of true hearts revealing.

And hark ! from the joyous infant choir,
　Which the Lord to His arms hath taken,
Notes sweet as breathe from the trembling lyre
　That the softest touch doth waken !
And from childhood's band who, when life's
　　　fresh glow
On their early bloom was lying,

Felt the shaft of death to their young hearts go,
  And His love enfold them dying !

So onward, long as the queenly moon
  Shall float through the azure nightly,
Or the sun ascend to his throne at noon,
  Or the evening star burn brightly,
Shall the choral hymn of the saints resound
  That chants of the Cross the story ;
It shall rise and blend with the trumpet's sound
  When the Lord shall come in glory !

THANKSGIVING.

NOVEMBER! draped in sullen gray,
  And veiled with withered leaves,
One ever-welcome, smiling day,
  Thy leaden gloom relieves.

Day of bright-hours, that all too fast
  With noiseless feet go by,
Oh, give me back the buried past
  Ere thou thyself shalt die!

Let me tread o'er the misty track
  Of long, long vanished years;
Let childhood's dreamy days come back
  With all their smiles and tears.

On memory's canvas, fair and bright,
  The dear old home is drawn,

And o'er it falls the golden light,
    As of a cloudless morn.

I see the trees that hemmed it round,
    On which, each year anew,
The robin built her nest and found
    A greeting warm and true.

I see the crib with ripened corn
    And yellow grain o'erflow,
The well-filled barn, the close-grazed lawn,
    The orchard's tempting glow.

I pass again the threshold where,
    A bounding child. I played ;
When parents, brothers, sisters, there
    For me an Eden made.

I see again my father's smile ;
    I hear my mother's song ;
Sweet dream ! so sweet, that still awhile
    I would the bliss prolong.

But onward hastes my restless thought,
   As onward trod my feet,
When, home and childhood left, I sought
   The strifes for manhood meet.

E'er since a man, with busy men,
   I've trod life's flinty path,
With crimsoned footsteps now, and then,
   Amid the tempest's wrath ;

Thou, loving God, my feet hast kept,
   That else afar had strayed :
Hast dried the tear when sorrow wept,
   And lit the gloomy shade !

Thy hand, o'er all the desert waste.
   My cup hath daily filled ;
The Bread of Heaven hath made me taste,
   And every wish hath stilled.

Though childhood's lights and joys can greet
   No more my fond return,

Homeward, each year, shall turn my feet,
    Long as life's flame shall burn.

Round the old hearth-stone met again,
    The old deep love shall glow,
And youthful mirth shall wake and reign,
    And hearts together flow.

Oh, ever-welcome, ever dear,
    Thou ancient festal day,
When Home calls back to social cheer
    Its wanderers long away.

THE SCEPTIC.

OH, pity the poor doubter darkly driven,
  He knows not whither. o'er life's troubled
    main ;
On sun and stars, to light the wanderer given,
  His eyes, now half bedimmed, are turned in
    vain.

No needle points for him the dubious way ;
  No friendly chart guides o'er the trackless
    deep ;
No lighthouse greets him with its gladsome ray ;
  No haven welcomes when wild tempests sweep.

The voice divine within he heedeth not ;
  The book of nature he doth all misread ;
Celestial Truth denied, her words forgot,
  Illusion cheats him and false lights mislead.

In fond conceit he dreams ere long to find,
  By his own wisdom led, a region fair,
Where placid streams adown sweet valleys wind,
  And days serenely glide without a care.

Ah, no! though many a blooming realm there be,
  Where beauty smiles beneath a cloudless sun,
Yet such fair shore his eye shall never see,
  Misfortune's victim ere his course be run.

His fated bark, long tossed the ocean o'er,
  At last shall founder helpless and alone;
Or stranded on some rugged, surf-beat shore,
  O'er him, in woful dirge, the waves shall moan.

Thou that hast faith, on God's good Word hold
      fast;
  Thy chart and compass both His truth shall be,
Till, reached thy port and all thy perils past,
  In peace thou floatest on the crystal sea.

SONG — THE WIFE.

WHEN through dark wilds and doubtful
    mazes,
  O'er thorny paths perplexed I rove,
And many a luring meteor blazes,
  And patience many an hour hath strove ;
When worn with care, my spirit sinking,
  No more elastic, strong and free,
Despondency's sad draught is drinking,
  And hopes like fading shadows flee ;
Oppressed, half weary of my life,
Thou art my solace, faithful wife !

Like some lone spot of verdure springing,
  The desert's dreary waste to cheer,
Which, chance the weary wanderer bringing,
  Yields soft repose by fountains clear ;
E'en thus, on earth's wide desert smiling,
  Appears my home, one fairer spot,

Where joy springs fresh each care beguiling,
  And noise and discord enter not ;
Of home, bright resting-place of life,
Thou art the soul, my noble wife !

When, duty's urgent call obeying,
  I wander from that home and thee,
My truant thought is ever straying'
  Backward thy gentle face to see ;
And when again my footsteps turning
  Bear me thy warm embrace to meet,
That thought with fond impatience burning
  Sweeps onward than the wind more fleet,
And stays not till, life of my life,
It rests with thee, my charming wife !

When comes at length the hour of meeting,
  I give and take the fervent kiss ;
Oh, with the thrill of such a greeting,
  Can earth compare another bliss ?
The joy of that eternal union
  That ransomed spirits round God's throne

Unites in heaven's own blest communion,
  Excels it, but excels alone ;
That be it mine, to endless life,
With thee to share, my angel wife!

MIDSUMMER NIGHT.

O'ER the dim, empurpled mountains,
   Fades the ruby light away ;
Shadows sleep where late the fountains
   Sparkled 'neath the glance of day.

Tranquil streams that, smoothly gliding,
   Mirrored tree and cliff and cloud,
All their placid beauty hiding,
   Gathering night-shades now enshroud.

Flowers that in the jocund morning
   Drank with blushing lips the dew,
Folded wait another dawning,
   And their wasted sweets renew.

Hurrying life's last murmur dying,
   Stillness broods o'er vale and hill,
Startled only by the crying
   Of the wakeful whip-poor-will.

Spirit of the peaceful hour,
   Now while nature sinks to rest,
Let thy sweet, subduing power,
   Still each passion in my breast!

Give calm thoughts of tasted sorrows,
   Tender memories wake again,
Bring me dreams of bright to-morrows,
   Hopes that shall not all be vain.

While with darkness vigils keeping,
   Here I linger silent, lone,
Come there, like the soft wind sweeping,
   Breathings from the realm unknown.

As yon watching stars above me
   Greet me, though afar they roll,
May not those in heaven that love me,
   Speak in whispers to my soul?

As if some new sense possessing,
   May I not those whispers hear?
Catch from airy lips a blessing,
   Know that holy ones are near?

Night's deep shade the world concealing,
   Makes the soul's quick glance more keen ;
In serener light revealing
   To her eye the things unseen.

Sights of unthought glory hidden,
   Sounds unheard by mortal ear,
Are not to her sense forbidden
   When she wakes to see and hear.

Beauty greets her, ever vernal,
   Melodies for earth too sweet,
Glows for her the Throne Eternal,
   Of Incarnate Love the seat !

On my spirit heavenward turning,
   Falls celestial grace like dew,
Waking all afresh her yearning
   Angels, to ascend to you !

Oh, while hushed is each commotion,
   While, my soul, thy thought is free,
Fervent breathe thy pure devotion,
   God and heaven are nigh to thee !

THE ANGEL CHILD.

THE seal of heaven was early set,
    Sweet child! upon thy sunny brow ;
Though lost to earth thou livest yet.
    All bright and glad I see thee now !

Those glowing eyes, that gentle smile.
    Spoke thee for earth a thing too fair ;
A cherub lent from heaven a while.
    A cherub's grace 'twas thine to wear.

Oft fondly beat a father's heart,
    To see thy budding life unfold ;
And oft a mother's tear did start,
    Born of deep yearnings all untold.

Hope dreamed that many a smiling year
    Should many a ripening charm display ;
But, oh! a voice we could not hear,
    Won thee in childhood's dawn away.

7

Yet, but in seeming didst thou die ;
  A joyous spirit, swift of wing,
'Twas thine to cleave yon azure sky,
  And, like the lark, to soar and sing.

Unquenched is that immortal fire !
  Dear child, thou didst not live in vain ;
And heaven shall grant our warm desire,
  To fold thee to our hearts again!

SONG.

GENTLY I glide, love,
  Glide o'er the deep;
Hushed are the wild winds,
  The proud billows sleep;
Soft gleams the summer moon
  On the still sea;
Yet roams my thought, love,
  It wanders to thee.

All, all is beauty,
  Around and above;
With me are kind hearts,
  And eyes beaming love;
Fair lips breathe music
  That charms the rapt ear,
But stirs not the soul, love,
  'Tis not thee I hear!

Where'er thou art, love,
    Peace fill thy breast!
Pure spirits guard thee,
    Awake or at rest;
When the morn breaketh,
    With breeze fresh and free,
Oh, may it bear, love,
    This fond heart to thee!

THE GOLDEN WEDDING.

'TIS fifty years! 'tis fifty years! how swiftly
    they have fled!
Since I thee, my best and dearest, to the bridal
    altar led!
In youthful grace and beauty thou wast blushing
    fresh and fair,
'Twas with pride and exultation that I stood
    beside thee there.

The hopes that then we cherished were the
    kindling hopes of youth ;
The vows which then we plighted were the vows
    of love and truth ;
And light before us glanced as we thought of
    coming days,
As when the summer sunbeam o'er the trembling
    water plays.

Of changeless bliss we dreamed not, for all too
    well we knew,
That athwart life's devious path many an unseen
    arrow flew ;
But we trusted that when wounded, when the
    bitter tear should start,
Sweet sympathy would heal, and cheat of half
    its woe the heart.

And we thought that should kind Heaven deign
    to smile upon our lot,
Grant a home and tranquil days in some dear
    secluded spot,
The flowers would seem more lovely and the
    stars shed purer light,
As we gazed on them together with reciprocal
    delight.

Now that fifty years are passed, and we cast a
    look behind,
What speaks the quick emotion that is rushing
    o'er each mind ?

Saith it of disappointment—of each vision empty
    found ?
Of hopes bright star declining and thick dark-
    ness gathered round ?

No, no, our thanks we offer to the gracious
    Hand that guides,
'Tis a placid stream that bears us, and peacefully
    it glides ;
May coming years thus greet us, till life's latest
    sands are run,
And life's close be like the twilight when has
    set a cloudless sun.

www.ingramcontent.com/pod-product-compliance
Lightning Source LLC
Chambersburg PA
CBHW032155010726
47493CB00008BA/2707